T0182619

Who Is
Shaun White?

by Shawn Pryor

illustrated by Andrew Thomson

Penguin Workshop

For Deon & Skyler Williams—SP

For Rhia, Cerys, and Esme—AT

PENGUIN WORKSHOP
An imprint of Penguin Random House LLC, New York

First published in the United States of America by Penguin Workshop,
an imprint of Penguin Random House LLC, New York, 2024

Copyright © 2024 by Penguin Random House LLC

Penguin supports copyright. Copyright fuels creativity, encourages diverse voices,
promotes free speech, and creates a vibrant culture. Thank you for buying an authorized
edition of this book and for complying with copyright laws by not reproducing, scanning,
or distributing any part of it in any form without permission. You are supporting writers
and allowing Penguin to continue to publish books for every reader.

PENGUIN is a registered trademark and PENGUIN WORKSHOP is a trademark
of Penguin Books Ltd. WHO HQ & Design is a registered trademark
of Penguin Random House LLC.

Visit us online at penguinrandomhouse.com.

Library of Congress Cataloging-in-Publication Data is available.

Printed in the United States of America

ISBN 9780593750803 (paperback)   10 9 8 7 6 5 4 3 2 1 CJKW
ISBN 9780593750810 (library binding)   10 9 8 7 6 5 4 3 2 1 CJKW

The publisher does not have any control over and does not assume any responsibility
for author or third-party websites or their content.

Contents

Who Is Shaun White?

On February 17, 2010, the men's halfpipe final competition at the Winter Olympics was held on Cypress Mountain, in Vancouver, Canada.

In snowboarding, a halfpipe is a huge semicircular trench built out of heavily packed snow (or dirt covered in snow) to make ramp-like walls. Those walls can be as high as twenty-three feet!

Snowboarders surf these snowy walls, going from one side to the other. When they reach the top of a wall, while in the air, they perform tricks with their snowboards before landing back in the pipe.

Snowboarding events are held worldwide and have been a part of the Winter Olympics since 1998.

One of the contestants in the 2010 men's halfpipe competition was Shaun White, a five-foot-eight-inch-tall American snowboarder. Because of his exciting snowboarding moves and long red hair, he was nicknamed the "Flying Tomato."

Everyone was focused on what Shaun planned to do during his second run. No one else in the competition could beat his incredibly high first-run score of 46.8, so Shaun didn't even have to take his second turn. But he had something to prove: He wanted to make sure that everyone knew that he was the best in the world.

Standing at the top of the halfpipe, Shaun got ready for his second and final run. With a quick push, he flew down the slope quickly, raced to the other side, and became airborne, twirling multiple times before landing, then swooping up the other side of the pipe. Shaun twirled in the air again, completing his snowboarding tricks with ease! The crowd cheered him on as he landed and retook the air. It was during his last airborne move, though, that he amazed the entire world as he combined three and a half twists and two flips in the air with the snowboard strapped to his feet! On his perfect landing, the crowd roared!

The air trick he had successfully pulled off was called the Double McTwist 1260. This was the first time anyone had successfully attempted it in any competition. Because of this run, Shaun scored 48.4, beating his own previous high score of 46.8.

"I wanted a victory lap that would be remembered," said Shaun White after performing the Double McTwist 1260 and taking home the gold medal in the halfpipe for Team USA. "I achieved that." No other Olympic snowboarder at the time had accomplished such a tricky move.

This was only one highlight in Shaun White's historic career. He helped usher in a new era of athletes and helped make snowboarding the popular sport it is today. As a world record holder for the most Olympic gold medals by a snowboarder, he remains one of the sport's greatest superstars.

CHAPTER 1
Childhood

Shaun Roger White was born on September 3, 1986, in San Diego, California, to his parents, Cathy and Roger White. Shaun is the youngest of four children. His half-brother, Jesse, is seven years older than he is, and his sister, Kari, is two years older. He also has an older half-sister, Jessica.

When Shaun was still an infant, doctors discovered that he had more than one heart defect. He had open-heart surgery just after he was born. Shaun's first heart surgery was not successful, and at the age of eighteen months, he needed another surgery. During this time, Shaun's sister, Kari, was also dealing with health problems and required brain surgery. "From there it was just a whirlwind of Kari, Shaun, Shaun, Kari; they used to share the same crib in the hospital," said Cathy.

Because of all the problems with his heart and the surgeries he needed when he was still very young, it was thought that Shaun wouldn't be able to play any type of physical sports. The surgeries left him with a scar on his chest. He had to have routine checkups with the doctor to monitor the stress levels on his heart and to make sure that everything was okay. The stress tests were intended to show how much he could push his body before it affected his heart. After the stress tests were done and Shaun's health improved, at the age four he was allowed to engage in more physical play again. But he was told not to sit in hot tubs or go scuba diving, because those activities would not be healthy for his heart.

Shaun and Kari played together a lot as kids because they were close in age. "Shaun and I were the closest," says Kari. "I'd make him French toast after school and keep an eye on him."

Shaun and Kari White

Shaun was full of energy, and sometimes that would get him into trouble at home, because he was very fearless as a child.

He felt that overcoming his limitations worked to his advantage. He once told a group devoted to heart surgery survivors that "something about having this experience at a young age really put a fight in me."

One day, when Shaun was five, Roger brought home a skateboard ramp to put in the backyard. He had gotten it from a neighbor. Even at a young age, Shaun was not afraid to try the wildest stunts on it. He would dive off the ramp and onto the backyard trampoline. "I just remember being obsessed with being in the air," Shaun said. All those stunts showed his parents that he had great balance and athletic ability. "He had nerves of steel. I don't even think he feels pain sometimes," his mother recalled. Shaun was always pushing himself to go further, faster, and higher.

Shaun's mother was a waitress. His father worked for the San Clemente water department. His parents both had been very athletic when they were younger. Cathy's parents had been professional roller derby players. Roger was a very talented surfer. He had wanted to be a professional surfer, but his father was not supportive of him having that type of career. He tried to get Shaun into surfing at a young age. "Shaun was supposed to be a surfer," Roger said. "I put him on a boogie board when he was really young, about four years old." In fact, Shaun is named after professional surfer Shaun Tomson. Shaun's father hoped his son would follow in Tomson's footsteps.

As a child, Shaun surfed, played soccer, skateboarded, and went skiing with his family. They bonded around their time together, skiing and snowboarding in the mountains.

Shaun loved trying to do anything his brother, Jesse, did. Because Jesse loved to snowboard, Shaun became very interested in it. Snowboarding then became more important to him than skiing. And Shaun began to focus on it.

He remembered, "I was five when I started snowboarding. I was entered into competitions of snowboarding at seven. Everybody in the family snowboarded." Because Shaun was so young, his mother told him the only way he would be allowed to snowboard with Jesse was if he rode with what is known as a switch stance. This would help Shaun learn how to control his speed and balance. Riding "goofy" means your dominant foot is forward—most people are right-handed, so this would be the right foot. Riding with a "switch" stance means you're standing with the opposite foot than you would normally ride with forward. These terms are used in both skateboarding and snowboarding.

Shaun listened to his parents about the importance of understanding the technical skills of snowboarding. That helped him learn how to snowboard on the slopes. His mom believed that if he were to fall in the snow while learning how to snowboard, the snow would act as a form of padding—unlike the hard ground in skateboarding.

Although Jesse later said that it had taken

him about a week to master the switch stance, he remembered that it took Shaun only four runs down the slope. "It was incredible."

Because his parents worked full-time, the weekends were the best time for everyone to be together. It was a major commitment for the family to go snowboarding every weekend, but they all enjoyed the time they spent together.

History of Snowboarding

The first snowboards were invented by Sherman Poppen in 1965. Sherman was an engineer and created the snowboard for his children. He joined two skis together and attached a rope to one end so a person could have some steering control as they stood on the board and glided down a hill. He called it the Snurfer.

Sherman Poppen

Seven years later, Dimitrije Milovich helped the snowboard to evolve. As a college student, Dimitrije was known for sliding down snow-covered campus hills using cafeteria trays. Wanting something better, he designed his own snowboard, which he nicknamed the Winterstick. His snowboard design is very similar to the snowboards that we see today. Dimitrije decided to leave college and move to Utah, where he created his own snowboard business, called Winterstick.

GNU snowboards were created by Mike Olson and Pete Saari in the United States, in 1977. During the 1980s Mike and Pete decided to start making snowboards specifically for women, which was a first. Jamie Anderson, one of the most medal-winning female snowboarders of all-time, used GNU snowboards during her career.

CHAPTER 2
Learning as a Family

Shaun and his siblings practiced snowboarding on the San Bernadino Mountains in Southern California, as much as a three-hour drive from their home. As fun as snowboarding can be, it is also an expensive sport, which requires equipment and tickets and passes to snowboard sites.

Shaun's parents did whatever they could to make sure that he and his siblings got to spend as much time as possible in the mountains learning the sport. When taking the lift to get to the top of the run, Shaun wasn't quite sitting in the chair securely. After his mother told him to stop, Shaun started to ride the lift safely.

Because the family couldn't afford to stay at

the resorts around the San Bernadino Mountains, they slept in their family van in the resort parking lots during winter weekends. They took the backseat out of the van and put a few beds down. This let them get to the mountains, snowboard, and save money at the same time. The also frequently traveled to Mount Hood in Oregon. "We used to camp out . . . in our family van. They had hot water at the rest stop, so we'd fill up, like, one milk jug to get wet and then a second jug to clean the soap off." There were times when the family had to bundle up in the van to stay warm at night, but they did their best to make the vehicle into a portable home.

Occasionally, the family would use the resort bathrooms to clean up in the morning and brush their teeth.

Shaun would snowboard all day, and then after he finished, he would skateboard until it was nighttime. He loved it. "I just remember going and going and never getting tired. It was so much fun."

Shaun was a fantastic snowboarder by age six, in part because he practiced so much. He began participating in amateur snowboarding tournaments. "My parents had taken a loan out on their home to pay for the snowboarding. I didn't come from a ton of wealth in the family, but with that came that fight." His mother contacted Jake Burton Carpenter, known as the Godfather of Snowboarding, and asked if his company would sponsor Shaun for his tournaments. He agreed. The company, Burton Snowboards, sponsored Shaun, who was only seven years old. Shaun now used a snowboard and snowboarding gear with the Burton brand name while competing. When he started to compete in more tournaments, his parents converted an old van into an RV so the family could travel and have a place to stay while on the road. At the age of seven, Shaun won his first competition!

Jake Burton Carpenter (1954–2019)

Born in New York City, Jake Burton was one of the inventors of the modern snowboard. He created the snowboard that riders like Shaun White and others use today. He started his snowboard manufacturing business in 1977 in a barn in Vermont. He would work as a caretaker of the horse barn during the day, make snowboards when he could, and then test the boards on his days off. Four years later, Burton Snowboards was a full-fledged business specializing in snowboards and snowboarding gear.

Over the next several years, Shaun dominated the amateur circuit, winning five national titles. In amateur tournaments, athletes who participate do not get paid to compete. Shaun was winning awards as an amateur athlete, but he wasn't earning money. In order to participate in professional events with the opportunity to win awards and money, a snowboarder has to join the United States of America Snowboard

and Freeski Association (USASA) and participate in USASA competitions.

The USASA hosts more than 500 snowboard and freeski events (skiing that involves tricks and jumps) yearly at almost 120 ski resorts across the United States. The season finishes at the USASA National Championship in Copper Mountain, Colorado. The National Championship lasts twelve days and more than

1,800 snowboarders and skiers participate in it. Shaun knew that eventually he was going to have to move to the professional world of snowboarding if he wanted to take his career to the next level.

CHAPTER 3
A Skating Accident

In addition to competing in snowboarding events, Shaun continued to compete in skateboard events and tournaments. In 1995, legendary skateboarder Tony Hawk became friends with Shaun at a skate park in Encinitas, California. "Tony was my hero and I was too terrified to talk to him, so every time I saw him at the skate park I would try to impress him with my skateboarding in the hopes that he would one day say something to me."

When Shaun was nine, Tony Hawk became his mentor, and in 1996 Tony took him on a professional skate tour across the country. The purpose of the tour was to highlight the skills and tricks of well-known skateboarders,

while also showing people that skateboarding was becoming a popular sport. Shaun's mother was guarded about her son hanging around athletes who were much older than he was, so she went on the tour to keep an eye on him. Shaun was the only child on the tour, which was sponsored by MTV, and MTV would air some of it on live television. This gave Shaun the chance to demonstrate his skateboarding skills in front of massive crowds and the world.

Shaun was ten years old when he joined the tour and was having a great time—until one event at the 1997 MTV Sports and Music Festival, where he was performing in a doubles-skating demonstration. Doubles-skating is when two skaters are on opposite ends of a large vertical pipe and they skate back and forth, past each other, while performing tricks. Shaun was skating doubles with legend Bob Burnquist, who was older, taller, and weighed much more than Shaun. As Shaun and Bob were about to begin, the TV announcer could be heard saying "You know, Shaun's really risking his life. Bob's got ten times the body mass Shaun does."

Bob Burnquist

Tony Hawk (1968–)

Tony Hawk was born in San Diego, California. He became a professional skateboarder at age fourteen and was eventually sponsored by Vans and Powell Peralta among other companies. He was nicknamed Birdman for the way he flew on a skateboard, and now owns a skateboard company called Birdhouse. Since 1999 he has also had a video game series named after him, with multiple titles and games released across all types of gaming consoles.

He is a legendary professional skateboarder and leader of the vertical skateboarding movement. He mentored many up-and-coming skateboarders and was the first to land a "900"—a trick that involves the completion of two-and-a-half mid-air revolutions on a skateboard. He retired from the world of professional skateboarding in 2003. Tony is also the founder of the Skatepark Project (formerly known as the Tony Hawk Foundation), which builds public skateparks in underfunded communities around the world to give all people a chance to skateboard. He is the most influential skateboarder of all time.

Moments later, they collided at full-speed, and Shaun's head and body hit the ramp very hard. He was on the ground, not moving at all. "It was the scariest moment of my life," said Cathy. "I thought we lost him." The medics put Shaun in an ambulance and quickly got him to the hospital.

The accident fractured Shaun's skull and broke his hand and his foot. These were the first major injuries that Shaun had ever had. After being hospitalized, he went back to school with two black eyes and a cast on what happened to be picture day. The teacher was shocked to see him bruised and wearing two casts. Some people in the school district disapproved of Shaun's parents because they felt that they were putting their son at risk. But Cathy and Roger knew that this was what Shaun loved doing and they wanted to support him.

For a lengthy period, Shaun lost the desire to skateboard. His mom didn't want him to become fearful and abandon the sport. After a few months, with the help of his mother, Shaun began skateboarding again. And when the winter came, it was time to snowboard again, too.

CHAPTER 4
Becoming a Pro Snowboarder

After healing from his horrific skateboarding accident and building up the courage to start skating again, Shaun had to begin practicing and training for another snowboarding season.

In 1997, Shaun had gotten to the point where he was well beyond much of the competition in amateur snowboarding. After years of competing on an amateur level, he decided to become professional. He was thirteen years old. From ages twelve through fifteen, he would repeatedly medal at USASA professional events. At thirteen, he began to travel the world to compete as a

snowboarder and started to earn money from his sponsorships. Unlike amateurs, professional snowboarders get paid to compete. It wasn't a lot of money, but it was enough to cover travel costs for the family so they could be together and watch Shaun's snowboard events. Shaun was younger than most of the people he competed against, so it suited him better to be with his family on the road.

Because Shaun was traveling so much, he missed a lot of school. To continue his education, he had to do independent study instead. Shaun had the same textbooks as he would have had in school as well as instructional packets. He turned in assignments to get his school credits. His mother always made sure that he completed his schoolwork and that he knew his grades were just as important as being a professional athlete. There were times when he would do his homework while on a plane heading to his next tournament. "I remember always feeling like I had to fight for what I was doing," he said. "We saw a future in this sport and others didn't, and I wanted to prove them wrong."

Snowboarding was becoming popular. More people were paying attention to the sport, making it even more profitable. Shaun won many tournaments and received more sponsorships and endorsements. His career as a professional was off to a great start.

In 2001, at the age of fifteen, Shaun became a millionaire from snowboarding. In 2002, at sixteen years old, Shaun won his first medals at the Winter X Games. He competed in the men's slopestyle and men's halfpipe. He won the silver medal in both events. In that same year, he also turned professional in skateboarding and became the Action Sports Tour Champion!

At the 2003 Winter X Games, Shaun won the gold medal in the men's snowboard slopestyle and halfpipe, and in the 2004 and 2005 games he won the gold medal in the men's slopestyle. He would later compete in the Summer X Games, earning two gold and silver medals and one bronze in skateboarding. He was the first athlete to compete in both the Summer and Winter X Games.

Throughout his teenage years, Shaun also participated on the amateur and professional skateboarding circuit, splitting time between sports during their respective off-seasons.

If it was the snowboarding off-season, Shaun would participate in skateboarding events. During the skateboarding off-season, he participated in snowboarding events.

The X Games

The first X Games were held in 1995, then under the name Extreme Games. The games feature competition in skateboarding, motocross, bicycle motocross (BMX), skiing, and snowboarding. Those who take part in the games have the chance to win gold, silver, and bronze medals, as well as prize money. The event was founded by ESPN (the Entertainment and Sports Programming Network) and featured on ESPN, ABC, and Disney-owned networks and services. Sponsors have included Monster Energy, Hot Wheels, Visa, and others.

The Summer X Games take place in August and are currently held in Austin, Texas. Competitive events in the Summer X Games are motocross, skateboarding, and BMX freestyle. The Winter X Games take place in January or February on Buttermilk Mountain in Aspen, Colorado. Events in the Winter X Games are big air skiing, slopestyle and superpipe skiing, big air snowboarding, snowboard slopestyle, and snowboard superpipe.

CHAPTER 5
The 2006 Winter Olympics

In 2001 Shaun fell short of qualifying for the 2002 Winter Olympics in Salt Lake City, Utah. But, on the run-up to the 2006 Winter Olympics in Torino, Italy, he won all four of the previous qualifying events. He put on a show with fantastic runs at the final qualifying event, giving him first place in the qualifier. He won all five qualifying events and was going to the 2006 Winter Olympics to represent the United States!

"I remember going to my first Olympics, and at this point I was nineteen years old, it was 2006. I just thought, like, 'Oh this would be cool, like, if I win.' You know, I don't think I knew the magnitude of it and so at the competition

I think I was a little too relaxed. I was really confident in myself," Shaun said, laughing. "I had this winning streak going in."

In the first qualifying run in the Olympic halfpipe, only the top six athletes from around the world make it to the finals. Shaun couldn't land the first hit (a trick done in the air) on his first run of the qualifier. Something inside of him woke up immediately after that run. He realized that he only had one more chance. If he didn't land in the top six, his Olympic dreams would be over. Shaun was nervous, but he reclaimed his focus and prepared for his second run. The pressure was on. He started his second run, hitting a massive live air trick for his first hit, and then made sure that he performed his other hits smoothly to qualify for the next round. He said, "Something about having to fight my way into the finals really set the tone for what was going to happen next."

In the finals, on his first run, Shaun was back

in the right mindset. He went up high for his first hit and got a lot of air for his second, grabbing his snowboard in midair and performing a beautiful 1080. Then, after doing a series of air-defying twists, he pulled off back-to-back 1080s and landed perfectly! His score of 46.8 was the highest of any competitor, giving him his first

Olympic win and the gold medal for the United States. Grabbing an American flag, Shaun started to wave it in the air as the crowd cheered him on.

His family was in the crowd, cheering and crying tears of joy. "It's a dream, right? It really is," said Roger. "It's making me wanna cry."

Olympic Snowboarding

To make the Olympic Snowboarding Team, you must participate in Olympic qualifying events. No more than the top four snowboarders can make the US Team in each event. There are five qualifying events for men and women, and one event for both men and women (mixed team snowboard cross). The most well-known event in Olympic snowboarding is the halfpipe. In the halfpipe event, snowboarders ride back and forth in a halfpipe structure and perform airborne tricks and turns (known as "hits") above the rim of the pipe. Snowboarders are then judged on the number of tricks, including height and speed of each, and on how well they perform. The highest scorer wins the gold medal, second-highest wins silver, and third-highest wins bronze.

All snowboarders must wear proper headgear and clothing in order to participate in the event. Anyone who is competing in a snowboarding event cannot stop moving in the halfpipe for more than ten seconds. If they do, they will be scored up to that point only, and they have to exit the halfpipe immediately. Unsportsmanlike behavior is strictly prohibited at all times.

After winning the Olympic gold medal, Shaun was interviewed and asked how he felt. He said, "I mean, it's been the best year of my life. It's amazing. I'm just happy my family's here."

The whole family rushed to hug Shaun. His mother, Cathy, told him: "You don't understand what you just did. You will be forever known as Shaun White, the Olympic gold medalist. That title will follow you for the rest of your life."

Shaun's old nickname, the "Flying Tomato," which was given to him by skateboarder Colin McKay, was used frequently in the broadcast, due to his long red hair, which flew from beneath his helmet as he sped down the pipe.

With this win, Shaun helped push snowboarding into the spotlight and helped give the sport the respect it deserved. The competition had over ninety million viewers in the United States alone. And it was just the beginning of an excellent career for Shaun.

Some Snowboarding Terms Explained

OLLIE: Using the tail of the snowboard as a spring

VERT: Short for *vertical*

AIR TO FAKIE: A type of trick where a rider rides straight up the wall, airs out, does not spin, and reenters the wall riding backward.

WHEELIE: Snowboarding with one tip of the board in the air

CORK: An off-axis rotation that vaguely resembles a corkscrew. The snowboarder rotates while upside down and angled.

NOSE AND TAIL ROLLS: Using the snowboard's nose or tail and spinning 180 degrees to change one's stance

DOUBLE CORK: Two full off-axis rotations (also known as inverts)

TRIPLE CORK: Three off-axis rotations (the most difficult type of cork)

How to Do the Double Cork

FRONTSIDE DOUBLE CORK 1080: Two head-over-heels flips with one full twist

DOUBLE McTWIST 1260: Three and a half twists and two flips in the air

1440: Four complete spin rotations in the air

FRONTSIDE TRIPLE CORK 1440: Four complete spin rotations and three off-axis flips in the air

CAB DOUBLE CORK: When a snowboarder hits the lip frontside at full speed, launches, and flips head over heels twice while rotating twice

1080: Completing three full spins and then landing smoothly

CHAPTER 6
Raising the Bar

In 2009, Shaun was preparing for the 2010 Winter Olympics. With the help of sponsors, he built a large private twenty-two-foot halfpipe near Silverton, Colorado. At the end of the halfpipe  was a massive foam pit. It allowed him to try risky tricks and land safely on the foam so that he could practice complex moves without hurting himself. The halfpipe was named Red Bull's Project X.

A group of professional snowboarders called the Friends Crew, which consisted of Danny

Davis, Luke and Jack Mitrani, Scotty Lago, and Mason Aguirre competed against Shaun at this time. When they heard about his private halfpipe, they asked sneaker company Nike to create a private halfpipe for them with an airbag at the bottom so they, too, could practice new tricks at the same level as Shaun.

From left, Danny Davis, Luke Mitrani, Scotty Lago, and Jack Mitrani

Shaun was attempting to elevate his snowboarding abilities and develop new tricks to win the halfpipe events at the next Olympics: "The goal of Project X was to invent new tricks, something that had never been done before. And in my mind, I had one trick that I really wanted to get. It was called the frontside double cork 1080"—three and a half twists and two flips in the air.

Several times, Shaun felt nervous or scared performing the unique trick, but he decided to face his fear and keep pushing forward. After some time and a lot of practice, he landed it! The trick was named the Double McTwist 1260. Shaun first performed it successfully at the Winter X Games in January 2010, winning the gold medal. It was his tenth appearance at the Winter X Games.

After qualifying for the 2010 Olympic Snowboarding Team, Shaun and the other American athletes headed to Vancouver, British Columbia, in February for the Winter Games. Shaun had become a major star athlete, and the world was watching to see if he could take the gold in the halfpipe again.

After making it to the halfpipe finals, Shaun's hard work paid off. His hits were so much higher than the other snowboarders, making flips and tricks with the greatest of ease. On his first run, he scored 46.8 out of 50! No other snowboarder could come close to Shaun's score after their second runs, which gave him the gold medal. But Shaun had one run left. Even though he had already won the gold, something weighed on him. He wanted the entire world to know that he was the best. He didn't want to simply take a victory lap—he wanted to make a statement.

Shaun made more than a statement on his second run as the world witnessed him pull off a Double McTwist 1260, the first in Olympic history. What a victory lap! The crowd cheered in amazement as he finished his run. "It was more about leaving my mark; this wasn't a fluke from the last Olympics," he said. "I'm here, and I've stayed on top, and look where I am now." Shaun had won back-to-back gold medals at the Winter Olympics. He was just twenty-four years old.

CHAPTER 7
A Major Comeback

During the 2014 Winter Olympics in Sochi, Russia, many believed that Shaun would bring home the gold medal for the United States as he had in the previous two Winter Games. He was to compete in the inaugural slopestyle contest, and in the halfpipe.

Shaun decided to pull out from competing in the slopestyle. He didn't want to risk injury in his quest to win the halfpipe for the third consecutive time and become the seventh person to win three straight gold medals in an individual event at the Winter Olympics.

Unfortunately, he placed fourth in the halfpipe event, failing to medal. It was the first time that the United States was shut out in the halfpipe since the sport was introduced to the Olympics in 1998. "I'm disappointed," said Shaun.

In October 2017, Shaun, now thirty-one, was training to compete in the next Winter Olympics, which would be held in South Korea. He decided to train in Cardrona, New Zealand, on an Olympic-size halfpipe, which stands twenty-two feet high and sixty-four feet wide from lip to lip.

Mount Cardrona, New Zealand

While attempting to perform a cab double cork 1440 trick, in which a snowboarder flips twice on a diagonal while spinning four times in the air, Shaun was hurt very badly. He had slammed his face on the rim of the halfpipe! He suffered cuts, gashes, and heavy damage to his forehead, nose, and lip. He would've been hurt even worse if he hadn't been wearing his helmet while training. Shaun had to be helicoptered from the training area to the closest hospital, almost two hundred miles away. Once he arrived at the hospital, he had surgery to close the wounds on his face. He required more than sixty stitches and had to stay in the hospital for five days. Shaun shared his after-surgery photo on social media.

It would take him a while to recover, and he was not yet a lock to make the 2018 US Olympic Snowboarding Team. He hired a physical therapist and a trainer to help him get stronger, which changed how he prepared for snowboarding events.

Shaun White and physical therapist Esther Lee

At this point, Shaun was third overall in the first qualifier but had failed to make the final, and finished fourteenth overall in the second qualifier. To have a spot on the team, he would have to do very well in his last two qualifiers—but first, he needed to heal before snowboarding again.

After fully recovering from surgery, Shaun was successful in his two final qualifiers. He was now on the 2018 men's Olympic Snowboarding Team representing the United States in Pyeongchang, South Korea. Shaun was on a mission to take home a medal in the halfpipe after a disappointing 2014 Winter Olympics, where he came in fourth. Now he felt he had something to prove.

Shaun performed very well during his first run in the final round of the halfpipe event, performing a frontside 1440, a lot of rotations in the air, a 1260 move, and very clean landings. For a moment, he held an early lead. But a new, younger snowboarder from Japan named Ayumu Hirano reclaimed the lead on his second run after performing back-to-back 1440s, putting Shaun in second place before his second run. On that run, Shaun fell and received a low score from the judges, keeping Ayumu in first place. With one round left, Shaun knew he would have to have a fantastic and flawless run to beat Ayumu and win the gold medal.

In the final round, Ayumu went first, trying to improve his high score

Ayumu Hirano

of 95.25, but he fell during the run. His 95.25 high score remained intact as Shaun prepared to take his turn. He would have to get a score higher than Ayumu's to win.

Shaun stood at the top of the halfpipe. Leaning forward, he started to race down and then up the pipe. Flying above the pipe, he began performing many complex tricks and landed every single one as the crowd cheered him on! He started with a frontside double cork 1440, landed perfectly, went back up, and pulled off a cab double cork 1440! He had never successfully landed a cab double cork 1440 in his career until this moment.

The crowd continued to cheer as Shaun finished his run. He patiently waited to see his score. The judges gave him a 97.75 score—enough overall points to win his third gold medal in the Winter Olympics! Once Shaun saw the score, he excitedly threw his snowboard in the air and screamed in celebration. He fell to his knees and began to cry. Then he hugged his mother.

Shaun said, "I was so overwhelmed with happiness, I've been through so much to get here. I had this crazy injury in New Zealand where I busted my face open. I actually did the same trick that injured me here in the halfpipe today. So there were a lot of obstacles to overcome and now it's all worth it."

Shaun's gold medal was also the one hundredth medal for the United States in Winter Olympics history. And in addition to competing in the Winter Olympics and the X Games at this time, Shaun was also participating in the International Ski Federation (FIS) World Cup competitions.

The FIS World Cup

The FIS World Cup is run by the International Ski Federation and is the top international skiing and snowboarding competition outside of the Olympics.

The federation was founded as the International Skiing Commission in 1910. They organize and oversee world cup competitions and world championships. The event is held in either February or March.

Shaun White won the snowboarding gold medal in the halfpipe in the 2018 FIS World Cup, and took home the bronze in 2017 and 2022.

CHAPTER 8
The Mission to Qualify

In late 2021, Shaun began training for his final Winter Olympics. The training took place in the Saas Valley in Switzerland. At around ten thousand feet above sea level, this was one of the highest-elevated camps that Shaun had ever trained at. After he finished his practice runs, he would hike all the way back up the halfpipe. At such a high altitude, this takes a lot of training and endurance. In his first Winter Olympics in 2006, Shaun was nineteen years old and one of the youngest competitors in snowboarding events. Now thirty-five, he was the oldest competitor. He said, "I can feel that nervous tension starting to begin, when I know what's looming in the distance and I just want to be ready."

Saas-Fee Mountains

Shaun completed many practice runs each day to get his routine of tricks just right. The competition would be more challenging than ever. "It's one of the only sports where there's no real template to follow," he said. Shaun was also dealing with some knee pain, but the high altitude and training started to make him and his knee feel better. As a safety measure, a massive, inflated landing pad was placed near the bottom of the halfpipe.

One of Shaun's biggest challengers was snowboarder Ayumu Hirano, who won the silver medal in the halfpipe in the 2018 Winter Olympics. "When I first started snowboarding, Shaun was like a superhero on TV," said Ayumu.

"It was seeing him on TV that inspired me to start competing." With so many snowboarders performing triple corks successfully, Shaun had his work cut out for him.

Forty-nine days before the 2022 Winter Olympics, Shaun competed in the Dew Tour Halfpipe in Copper Mountain, Colorado. It was the second qualifying event for the Olympic Snowboarding Team. Shaun had made it to the finals. In these, the remaining snowboarders get three runs, and the highest score of the three runs counts. Shaun planned to get a high score on his first run and then make solid second and

third runs in order to make the Olympic team. At the Toyota US Grand Prix earlier that month, Shaun had said, "The biggest goal is to be the top finishing American, that's the key."

The 2021 Dew Tour Olympic qualifier course

Twelve American snowboarders participated in the event, and only four could make the United States team. Other snowboarders across the world competed as well. For the US snowboarders, the goal was to get on the podium, meaning finishing the event in first, second, or third place, or be an overall event point leader. Shaun was competing against people who looked up to him when he

Taylor Gold

was younger. "I remember going to the US Open when I was twelve. Shaun won that year and he signed my goggles," said Taylor Gold, a member of the USA Halfpipe Pro Team. "We grew up watching him when we were five, six years old. He was dominating already, so it's pretty surreal," said Lucas Foster, another USA Halfpipe Pro Team member.

Shaun knew that he was going to have to earn this.

On his first run, he got way up in the air and performed a 1440 and worked up to his signature Double McTwist 1260 before washing out completely, ending his first run.

For his second run, Shaun needed a great run to either beat the high score or place on the podium, and he washed out again after performing his first trick.

By his final run, Taylor Gold was in first place and a lock to make the team. Shaun was going to have to dig deep to succeed. He flew in the air for his first trick, landed another 1440, pulled off all of his tricks, and performed a complete and clean entire run.

But it wasn't enough for him to make the podium. He would have to continue participating in the qualifying events. At the final event, the Laax Open World Cup, Shaun finally qualified for the Olympic team. He realized, however, that this would be his last Winter Olympics and his final time as a professional athlete. His body was starting to age. He had been competing as an athlete since he was a young boy—and it now was taking a toll.

CHAPTER 9
The Final Olympics

At the 2022 Winter Olympics in Beijing, China, Shaun White, the three-time Olympic gold medalist and defending halfpipe champion, was ready. The competition was more challenging than ever, with snowboarders Ayumu Hirano from Japan, Scotty James from Australia, Jan Scherrer from Switzerland, and Taylor Gold from the United States among them. Even though Shaun was a champion snowboarder, he was now seen as the "thirty-five-year-old underdog" when compared to the other competitors, whose ages ranged from sixteen to twenty-eight years old.

Shaun knew he would have to get high scores on his halfpipe runs to keep up with the other

Scotty James   Jan Scherrer

top snowboarders. It was also freezing at the snow park where the event occurred, with temperatures as low as fifteen degrees. He had a poor first run, and had to make a terrific second run to get into the finals—which he did.

In the finals, after Shaun's first run on the halfpipe, he scored 72.0, keeping him in the competition. Shaun was very pleased. Scotty failed to land his opening tricks during their first halfpipe run, and even though Ayumu had landed the first triple cork in Olympics snowboard history during his first run, he also fell, hurting his overall score.

Ayumu Hirano

Shaun's second halfpipe run was fantastic. He performed a cab 1440, then pulled off back-to-back 1260s for an overall score of 85, putting him in second place behind Jan Scherrer, who had scored an 87.25. The possibility for him to get his fourth medal in the Winter Olympics was strong.

Scotty then followed up with a performance that earned him a leading score of 92.5, putting him in the possible position of winning the gold medal with one run left. Ayumu was incredible on his second run, performing a triple cork move and a cab 1440 to score a 91.75, moving him to second place and overtaking Shaun. With the round now over, Jan's score placed him a hair over Shaun for third place.

For his third and final run, Shaun knew that he had to get the highest score possible to place for a medal. From the top of the halfpipe, he was ready. He took off with incredible speed, and he knew that if he could stick a cab double-cork 1440, it could give him the score he needed to medal. As he flew into the air to perform the move, everything looked great until he attempted to land. And then he fell!

Shaun picked himself up from the ground and slowly snowboarded down the halfpipe while saluting the crowd and camera at his final competition. Ayumu scored a 96 on his last run, guaranteeing him the gold. Scotty took home the silver, and Jan took home the bronze. Shaun finished fourth in his final Winter Olympics. He was 2.25 points away from getting the bronze medal.

"I wish I would have done better in my runs," Shaun said. "I'm leaving behind a lifetime and a career in this sport and a legacy. And I'm proud of every bit, every moment. So thank you. Thank you, snowboarding. Thank you to everybody watching, and I can't wait for what's next."

CHAPTER 10
Life After Retirement

After Shaun finished in fourth place at the 2022 Winter Olympics, he retired from competitive snowboarding at age thirty-five. On February 18, 2022, he made his retirement public by posting it online for everyone to see.

Shaun wrote, "I slid down the halfpipe at the Olympics for the final time. Typing this makes me just as emotional as I felt last Friday. It brings me tears of joy. It has been a rollercoaster of emotions, and I am overwhelmed with appreciation. Closing this chapter of my life has made me reflect on the past 22 years as a professional snowboarder with gratitude."

Shaun retired as a five-time Olympian, winning three gold medals in the halfpipe competition. He is also a twenty-time medal winner of the Winter X Games, with nine gold medals in the superpipe competition, five gold medals in slopestyle competition, two silver medals in the superpipe and one in slopestyle competition, and three bronze medals in the slopestyle competition. He also earned five medals at the Summer X Games, competing in skateboarding events, and is a three-time FIS World Cup standings medalist in snowboarding.

Though Shaun was no longer competing in professional athletic events, he found a new path that would still keep him involved in snowboarding. A month before his final run at the 2022 Winter Olympics, he launched his active lifestyle and athletic brand, called Whitespace.

Whitespace released a line of outerwear, snowboarding equipment, and clothing. Shaun and his brother, Jesse, had created Whitespace together. Shaun also created a signature snowboard for the brand, which is black with a white stripe running down the middle, called the Whitespace Freestyle Shaun White Pro.

The idea for Whitespace had first started to form in 2018 after Shaun no longer had other brand sponsorships: "All these things came together; I had the thought of, instead of coming up with all these base graphics, I want to have our calling card be the white stripe. That's who we are. Whitespace is obviously a play on my name,

but also it means opportunity, a gap in the market, a blank canvas waiting for something new and creative. Snowboarding is one of the only sports where I can invent a new trick and be the best in the world. I love that opportunity and openness about the sport."

Shaun met actress Nina Dobrev during the 2012 Teen Choice Awards. He presented the Choice TV Show Sci-Fi/Fantasy award to the *Vampire Diaries* cast. Nina was part of the cast of that television show. It wasn't until several years later that they met again, this time at a conference

where they were both featured speakers. Afterward, the two went out for a meal together, and Shaun was surprised by the number of people who kept coming to their table asking for a picture with Nina. He said, "I actually didn't know anything about her. I was like, 'What's happening? What's going on?' It was actually really funny." The two got to know each other and have been dating since 2020.

In 2023, Shaun White published his autobiography, *Shaun White: Airborne*. In it, he shared his personal history as a professional and Olympic athlete.

Shaun has left an amazing mark in the world of sports. He (along with 2022 Olympic gold medalist Chloe Kim) is the face of snowboarding. He

Shaun White and Chloe Kim

is a pioneer of the sport, who also excelled at skateboarding, skiing, and high-flying, incredible tricks at the X Games. He has influenced generations of snowboarders and skateboarders with his highlights and award-winning legacy. He said, "Since I was six years old, I've been in the mix and watching snowboarding grow and change. I never would have expected it to go this far."

Shaun is an incredible athlete who helped take the world of snowboarding mainstream. He is popular among people of all ages and athletic interests. Most of all, he always made sure that he was having fun.

Timeline of Shaun White's Life

1986 — Shaun Roger White is born on September 3 in San Diego, California

1992 — Learns how to snowboard at age six

2002 — Wins silver medals in the slopestyle and superpipe in his first Winter X Games

2003 — Wins gold medals in slopestyle and superpipe at the Winter X Games

2004 — Wins gold medal in the slopestyle at the Winter X Games

2005 — Becomes the first athlete to participate in both the Winter and Summer X Games, winning gold in the slopestyle at the Winter X Games and silver in the skateboard vert event at his first Summer X Games

2006 — Wins the gold medal in the men's halfpipe at the Winter Olympics in Torino, Italy

2010 — Wins the gold medal in the men's halfpipe at the Winter Olympics in Vancouver, Canada

2018 — Wins the gold medal in the men's halfpipe at the Winter Olympics in PyeongChang, South Korea

2022 — Achieves a bronze in the halfpipe standings of the FIS World Cup

— Finishes fourth at the 2022 Winter Olympics in the men's halfpipe in Beijing, China

— Launches clothing and athletic brand Whitespace

Timeline of the World

1983	*Star Wars: Episode VI: The Return of the Jedi* movie released on May 25
1985	Wreck of the RMS *Titanic* is found in the North Atlantic Ocean by Robert Ballard
1990	The Hubble Space Telescope is placed in orbit
1996	Philadelphia receives a record thirty inches of snowfall on January 7, during one of the worst blizzards in US history
2003	Actor Arnold Schwarzenegger is elected governor of California on October 7
2005	Hurricane Katrina floods the city of New Orleans, Louisiana
2009	Barack Obama is sworn in as the forty-fourth president of the United States on January 20
2011	The final space shuttle mission is completed
2020	The Oakland Raiders football team moves to Las Vegas
2021	Olivia Rodrigo releases "Drivers License," a single that would go on to be streamed over a billion times
2022	Ketanji Brown Jackson becomes the first Black woman on the Supreme Court
2023	NFL quarterback Tom Brady announces his retirement from the NFL

Bibliography

*Books for young readers

*Abdo, Kenny. ***Shaun White***. Sports Biographies. Minneapolis: FLY!, 2022.

*Doeden, Matt. ***Shaun White***. Minneapolis: Lerner, 2012.

*Fitzpatrick, Jim. ***Shaun White***. World's Greatest Athletes. Parker, CO: Child's World, 2014.

*Hansen, Grace. ***Shaun White***. Abdo Kids Olympics Biographies. Minneapolis: Abdo Kids Jumbo, 2019.

*Scheff, Matt. ***Shaun White***. Extreme Sports Stars. Minneapolis: Sportszone, 2014.

Tollin, Mike, et al., executive producers. ***Shaun White: The Last Run***. HBO Max, 2023; 4 episodes.

White, Shaun. ***Shaun White: Airborne***. New York: Rizzoli, 2023.

Websites

www.cbsports.com

www.olympics.com